"Rejoice, young person, while you are young, and let your heart be glad in the days of your youth."
Wise King Solomon

DEVOTIONAL FOR YOUTHS

GROWING UP IN CHRIST

Terry Overton

DEVOTIONAL FOR YOUTHS

Growing Up In Christ

Terry Overton

Christian Publishing House
Cambridge, Ohio

Christian Publishing House

Professional Conservative Christian
Publishing of the Good News!

CPH Since 2005

Copyright © 2018 Terry Overton

Unless otherwise indicated, Scripture quotations are from the English Standard Version (ESV)

The Holy Bible, English Standard Version. ESV® Text Edition: 2016. Copyright © 2001 by Crossway Bibles, a publishing ministry of Good News Publishers.

DEVOTIONAL FOR YOUTHS: Growing Up In Christ

Authored by Terry Overton

This is a work of fiction. Names, locations, characters, and incidents are the product of the author's imagination.

ISBN-13: **978-1-945757-90-7**

ISBN-10: **1-945757-90-6**

Dear Readers:

This book of devotionals was written for some amazing young children and teens who sent texts to the author and asked for devotionals about particular topics. The devotionals were written and text back to the young Christians who received them within hours. These topics were requested because these individuals wanted to think about, from a Christian perspective, how to deal with challenges they were experiencing in their everyday lives. The topics included situations at school, home, and for the teenagers, even work. When these young Christians told their friends about the devotionals, their friends requested additional topics. For parents and grandparents who might be reading this introduction, here is the important message: **young Christians think a lot about how God wants them to handle situations.** They think about interactions with their peers, teachers, and others, and seek guidance from a Christian perspective. Young Christians may not always show that they are thinking about their faith, but they often are. The devotionals included in this book span a variety of topics that might be used for conversation starters and additional Bible Study. It is the author's hope that young Christians will find guidance between the pages of this book.

Table of Contents

Thankfulness

"Give thanks in all circumstances; for this is the will of God in Christ Jesus for you"
1 Thessalonians 5:18

Thankfulness is a great beginning topic. It is a concept that immediately puts us in a good mood. We are always thankful for our blessings, such as our parents, brothers, sisters, a home to sleep in, and food to eat. It is easy to be thankful for the good things.

But God also tells us to be thankful for all circumstances. When you think about it, that means be thankful for exams in school, be thankful for the bad grade you made on an assignment and be thankful for "mean" teachers. Why in the world should we be thankful for these things? Of course, all of these will help us learn and have better futures. So, that is not too hard to understand.

Even more difficult, how do we be thankful for a "friend" that we are currently having a fight with? Or one that is not truthful? These are harder. We have to think a little more about how this works. These situations are tests for us to be better Christians. These challenges will require us to stretch our brains and think about how we can resolve these issues like Jesus would expect us to do. It turns out; these tests are also the kinds of situations that make us better in the future. Know this: **God will not give you more**

than you can handle. He has already blessed us with the ability to stop and think about situations before we react so that we can be a good example to the other people. If you are in a situation that seems too difficult to handle by yourself, talk to your parents, grandparents, Sunday school teacher, or other adult and ask for help. And always pray. Talk to God just like a friend and let Him know you want His help.

> *"And whatever you do, in word or deed, do everything in the name of the Lord Jesus, giving thanks to God the Father through him" Colossians 3:17*

Don't Sweat the Small Stuff

"Peace I leave with you; my peace I give to you. Not as the world gives do I give to you. Let not your hearts be troubled, neither let them be afraid" John 14:27

"Out of my distress I called on the Lord; the Lord answered me and set me free. The Lord is on my side; I will not fear. What can man do to me?" Psalm 118:5-6.

It is so easy for us to live at an almost manic pace of life. Why? And what does that mean? Our worlds move too fast these days. We have to go to so many places, complete so many responsibilities, maintain good grades or perform well at work, and through all of this, we have to smile and be nice to others, always. (Even when others may get on our nerves!) Our world demands that we do these things. This is the status quo. The way the world works right now. And what do we do in our "down time" when we are not at school or work? We are running all around doing things, being bombarded by media, social media, texts, messages, phone calls, invitations, events, sporting outings, and on and on. And when we are home; there are responsibilities there too! Laundry, dishes, chores, etc.

What should we do? The first verse above reminds us that Jesus left us with peace. He gave us the peace of mind of knowing that no matter whatever else happens, we all have been given His grace. The first passage also says the peace He gives is not like the peace of the world. His peace through grace is even better! Because He has given this to us, we should not worry or be troubled about all of the other worldly things. He said we should not be afraid.

So how in the world can we keep from stressing about the small stuff? How can we have peace when everything around us moves at such a crazy and demanding pace? The answer is in the second verse. We should call on God. Know this: **Because we have Him on our side, we can overcome anything the world tosses our way.** The trick is, always depend on God. Depending on God means it is like He is walking right beside you. He is always there. Your responsibility is to remember that He is always with you. His hand is outstretched to you—grab it when you are feeling anxious about anything. Take a breath. Close your eyes. And remember, He sees the world differently from His view. From His view, our world surely looks very small and we must look like a bunch of ants! Our worries about day-to-day demands are "small stuff" compared to God's plan for us.

"Cast your burden on the Lord, and he will sustain you: he will never permit the righteous to be moved" Psalm 55:22

Growing Your Faith

"Now faith is the assurance of things hoped for, the conviction of things not seen" Hebrews 11:1

"For by grace you have been saved through faith. And this is not your own doing; it is the gift of God" Ephesians 2:8

In our world today, we can see anything we want to see on the internet. We can marvel at video clips of nature that are from countries halfway around the globe while we are sitting in our living room. We can virtually experience just about anything we want to see or hear because of the advancements in technology. But as the first verse above tells us, faith is for the things we hope for that we cannot see. We must have a conviction or a belief. In order to believe in God, we must have faith because we cannot see Him. Every single day, we see the evidence of God: the wind blows, the waves of the ocean move water to the shore, beautiful butterflies float in the air, scaly looking miniature monsters (lizards) scuttle about, animals move about the earth, babies are born, toddlers learn to walk. These are all evidence of God although we cannot see Him. We have faith; we know He is there always.

Having faith in God also means that we are given God's grace or forgiveness. He did not have to give us this grace; He wanted to give us grace because He loves us. He knows that we are undeserving and yet, He wants us to have this love and grace. The only thing we need to do is have faith in God and His Son, Jesus Christ who gave us this grace on the cross.

How do we increase our own faith? That is easy. We can increase our faith by reading and studying the word of God.

"So faith comes from hearing, and hearing through the word of Christ" Romans 10:17

The Bible is the living word of God. Know this: **God reveals to us different ways that we can apply the meaning[1] from the Bible at different times in our lives.** We will understand exactly what the author meant to convey by reading the verses and using good study tools. One verse can be applied entirely different to you five years from now. It will have the application that you need. This means you can increase your faith your whole lifetime. Isn't that a wonderful gift? It is like opening a different present each time you read the verses.

---

[1] Each Bible verse has only one meaning, which is what the author meant by the words that he used. There are not different meanings each time you read a verse; there are different ways that you can apply what the author meant. Do not read your 21st-century mindset into the Bible but rather take out what the author meant and correctly apply it into your 21st-century life.

Jesus Will Return

"For you yourselves are fully aware that the day of the Lord will come like a thief in the night" 1 Thessalonians 5:2

"But concerning that day and hour no one knows, not even the angels of heaven, nor the Son, but the Father only" Matthew 24:36

We know that Jesus died on the cross and arose on the third day. We have read verses that tell us the details of that first reappearance and also about the days that followed. Have you ever wondered how the disciples must have felt? First, they witnessed the wondrous miracles that He showed his followers in his short time here on earth. That must have been amazing! Then, His disciples saw Him tortured and killed. How their hearts must have broken. And how they must have rejoiced when he appeared to them on the third day. He even came again to make certain each one of the disciples fully understood that, for the rest of their lives, they were to teach others about the ultimate grace of God and that Jesus would return again.

We are now waiting for His return. The most important thing to remember is that we are to be ready and that no one, even Jesus, knows when that day will occur. So, what do we do in the meantime? We prepare. Like the first passage states above, the Lord will arrive just like a thief in the night, to our great surprise on that day. What a wonderful surprise that will be!

"Therefore you also must be ready, for the Son of Man is coming at an hour you do not expect" Matthew 24:44

How do we prepare? We make certain we are in good standing with God by asking forgiveness when we make mistakes. We read the Scriptures. We try hard to follow the commandments. We take care of each other following the examples of Jesus. Know this: **we should use the gifts, given to us by God, to live a life that follows the right path and we are to help others along the way.**

"For we are his workmanship, created in Christ Jesus for good works, which God prepared beforehand, that we should walk in them" Ephesians 2:10

Think about the many gifts that God has given to people. He planned these gifts for you to use for His glory. Some people have the gift of musical talent. Some people have a gift of being great athletes. Others have a gift of painting, teaching, speaking to large groups, or writing. These are all gifts that can be used to bring others to know God. What are your gifts and how can you use them?

When You Are Scared

"For God gave us a spirit not of fear but of power and love and self-control" 2 Timothy 1:7

"Fear not, for I am with you; be not dismayed, for I am your God; I will strengthen you, I will help you; I will uphold you with my righteous right hand" Isaiah 41:10

God created humans to have emotions of all sorts: happiness, anger, frustration, sadness, fear, excitement, anxiety, and love, to name a few. We are blessed to have so many wonderful emotions that we can experience every day. Think what it would be like to go through every single day feeling exactly the very same way all day long. That would be so boring! But notice what the first verse says about our spirit. Remember that God gave you a spirit that is not of fear, but of power! And not only that, our spirits are for love and also self-control. Let's think about that for a minute. The spirit we are all blessed with has the power to be brave. How do we know this? Because God states that our spirit also has self-control. This means that we can use our spirit to control fear and other feelings.

Emotions are definitely influenced by our own thinking. You think about something exciting (like Christmas, a birthday party, or the cute new student in school!) and you feel excitement. Think about something you are having difficulty with, like algebra or English literature, and you feel frustration before you even start your homework! By thinking fun or positive, happy thoughts, our happy or excited emotions will follow. If you think about something you have to do that is scary, you will feel afraid before the day you have to do that scary thing. So, the first part of the emotion about something in the future is actually the thought about that future event. Here is where that self-control comes in very handy. It might seem hard to do at first, but you can do it! Control your thoughts. Think about positive things. If something is scary, think about how God is right there beside you and supporting you. Sometimes, you might think about Him actually putting His arm around you to give you strength. You can imagine how that strong arm would feel around you, helping you to be brave. The second verse above tells us exactly that. The verse says that God will give us strength and even hold us up with His right hand. Of course, we have to ask Him for help. So, what better way to take your mind off of the scary event than to say prayers to God asking him to give you strength? The whole time you are in the actual scary event, say prayers over in your mind and feel His presence. Know this: **If you are praying, He will be there!**

"I sought the Lord, and he answered me and delivered me from all my fears"
Psalm 34:4

Remain Steadfast in Your Faith

"The wind blows where it wishes, and you hear its sound, but you do not know where it comes from or where it goes. So it is with everyone who is born of the Spirit."
John 3:8

"Jesus said to him, 'Have you believed because you have seen me? Blessed are those who have not seen and yet have believed'" John 20:29

"You are the light of the world. A city set on a hill cannot be hidden. Nor do people light a lamp and put it under a basket, but on a stand, and it gives light to all in the house. In the same way, let your light shine before others, so that they may see your good works and give glory to your Father who is in heaven" Matthew 5:14-16

Holding steadfast to your faith can be challenging at times. So many demands, exciting things happening in school, and exciting things happen in your social life every day! The first verse tells us that the Holy Spirit is within us and that the Holy Spirit may help to take us in many directions to do many things in the future for God. Sometimes we may not feel like our faith is out in front of everything we do, but, because we already have the Spirit within us, it is always there. Maybe the Spirit is like a computer program that is running in the background while you are actually working on a different webpage. It is still there, still on, and waiting for you to get back to that program when you are ready. The Spirit, once it is in you, will be there. There may be a time in your life when you have something happen that causes you to question God. Even when you are questioning, God is still there within you...waiting.

Did you know that Jesus talked about you? The second verse tells us that He was already thinking about us! He knew that, since we had not seen him in our lifetime (at least not yet!), we might have a harder time with faith. He also blessed us specifically because we do believe! How cool is that?

But the third verse is the most telling one about keeping your faith strong. When you are ready, you will be shining your light of faith in the world. You might shine this light by: helping a friend, helping your parents and siblings, loving animals and people, being a Christian first in your future professional life, being a shining example of a Christian wife, husband, and parent, and shining your faith light for others to see as you help point them to the cross.

You can boost your faith by remembering that we are all born again in Christ. **Know this: we all have a second chance and we all will be with Him for eternity.** That gets me excited just thinking about it!

If you find yourself in a slump, you can always turn to the Bible for inspiration or just to get your mind thinking about faith. It is a good way to jump start your heart and mind back to your faith and training your belief.

"All Scripture is breathed out by God and profitable for teaching, for reproof, for correction, and for training in righteousness" 2 Timothy 3:16

Use Only Kind Words

"Gracious words are like a honeycomb, sweetness to the soul and health to the body" Proverbs 16:24

"Let no corrupting talk come out of your mouths, but only such as is good for building up, as fits the occasion, that it may give grace to those who hear" Ephesians 4:29

We go through challenges every day. We experience struggles, frustration, and even anger in certain situations. Sometimes these struggles are just within us over something we are trying to do, but we are having difficulty. We might be struggling with a school assignment, a chore, or work. In these situations, we are experiencing frustration within and not due to an interaction with someone else. Sometimes we might become so angry that we use language that we would not use if Jesus was standing in the room. But of course, He is everywhere! He knows of our shortcomings and our sin but easily forgives us when we ask. The Bible reminds us that kind words are the best and that even our own physical and mental health will be better if we control our angry thoughts and words.

There are other struggles or occasions in which we are interacting with others. These interactions may become unpleasant because we are frustrated, or it might become unpleasant because the other person is having a frustrating or angry experience.

The words might fly out of your mouth before you know it! Again, we can ask forgiveness.

How can we better follow the examples of Jesus? It is especially difficult when things happen so fast that we feel we don't have time to think before our lips react. But we should make every attempt to do so. The first verse below reminds us that we can take control of every thought. And the second verse points out that our words are very powerful. Know this: **our words can help others in significant ways that we may not even know.**

> *"We take captive every thought to make it obedient for Christ" 2 Corinthians 10: 5*

> *"Your words have upheld him who was stumbling, and you have made firm the feeble knees" Job 4:4*

How can we focus on using good words? How can we help others to be kind? We must lead by example. We must first use kind words and interact in thoughtful ways to help each other. When another person hears your kind language and experiences your helpful actions, they will be more likely to do the same to you.

> *"Therefore encourage one another and build one another up, just as you are doing" 1 Thessalonians 5:11*

Reading the Word of God

"Your word is a lamp to my feet and a light to my path" Psalm 119:105

"Heaven and earth will pass away, but my words will not pass away" Matthew 24:35

"The grass withers, the flower fades, but the word of our God will stand forever" Isaiah 40:8

You have been taught, and probably read, that the Bible is the living word of God. They are living because the Bible has continued to inform people about God for thousands of years and is just as meaningful now. These words live because they are interpreted by you according to your own circumstances at the time. God knows what you will need. He also uses these words to interject the Holy Spirit into the reader. This is how God wants it to be. He wants us to read the words and interpret the help and meaning that we need at different times of our lives. The Spirit helps us to feel the meaning.

The passages above remind us that the word of God is written to guide us, and these words will always be there. When we have so many things going on in our lives, it feels like we don't have time to read the Scriptures and think about God. But, since the words are our guide, they can make our lives easier and more blessed. The words can help us get along better with others around us and can help us to learn how to be an example to others.

> *"So faith comes from hearing, and hearing through the word of Christ"* *Romans 10:17*

Since the words of God strengthen our faith, it is important for us to make time to read the verses. But the Bible contains 66 books with numerous chapters within each book! Wow! That is a lot of reading! How do you know where to start? If you have just a few minutes each day, how do you know what to read? There are different approaches to this. Some people begin with the New Testament because this tells us the words and story of Jesus. Others believe they should start at the beginning, with the Old Testament, and read all the way through. Since the only way to the Father is through the Son, starting with the New Testament first seems appealing. The Old Testament has a great deal of early history and the politics of the world from that era. These are important for us to understand so that we get the big picture of God and His work in the world. Other people prefer to read the songs and poetry (Proverbs, Psalms). These have great insight into your daily life, too. There is probably no best way to read the Scripture. Since it will have a different meaning every time you read it, year after year, it may not matter where you start. You can decide. And you don't have to read a great deal each day. It takes just a few minutes to read a couple of verses and those very verses might make the difference in your day. You can also read Scriptures within books or devotionals.

All of these are great ways to study. But don't punish yourself if you miss a day to two here and there. You can always catch up when you have more time on the weekends or other down times. Know this: **God is patient and will wait for you if He knows you have faith in Him.**

Sharing the Truth

"And he said to them, 'Go into all the world and proclaim the gospel to the whole creation. Whoever believes and is baptized will be saved, but whoever does not believe will be condemned'" Mark 16: 15-16

"Strive for peace with everyone, and for the holiness without which no one will see the Lord" Hebrews 12:14

One of the most amazing things in history that happened after Jesus ascended into Heaven was the quickness with which the word of Jesus spread all over civilizations shortly afterward. These disciples and believers were assisted by the Holy Spirit. Not only did the Spirit provide these early believers with strength and knowledge, but they were also endowed with a host of different languages to use as they went out to the spread the word. Imagine, in an instant, you know several different languages all at once without studying those languages! God knew that in order to spread the news of Jesus quickly, these believers would need these languages. Astonishing!

Today, how is the truth of God spread in your day-to-day life? Of course, people go to church. People read the Bible. Some people watch TV shows or movies about Jesus. But what is the average person expected to do to spread the word? For true believers, we are all given gifts from God that we can use to help others understand about God and His Son. Perhaps a person has a gift of singing, speaking, teaching, or writing. You may have heard that some are "called" by God to actively spend their lives teaching about God. In Jeremiah chapter 1, the Bible tells us about how Jeremiah was called:

> *"Now the word of the Lord came to me, saying, 'Before I formed you in the womb I knew you, and before you were born, I consecrated you, I appointed you a prophet to the nations'*
>
> *Then I said, 'Ah Lord God! Behold, I do not know how to speak, for I am only a youth'*
>
> *But the Lord said, 'Do not say I am only a youth for to all to whom I send you, you shall go, and whatever I command you, you shall speak. Do not be afraid of them, for I am with you to deliver you' declares the Lord" Jeremiah 1:5-8*

This tells us that Jeremiah was called and that God took care of him, prepared the way, so that Jeremiah could go out into the world and teach others. Know this: **God will give us what we need to tell others about Him.**

In everyday situations, we can also spread the word just by our examples that we show to others. In this way, they know your heart is true and that God is your guide. Spreading the word is something that we do, but the individual who is listening has the choice of agreeing and following God or rejecting the truth. As the passage at the beginning points out, those who reject the word will not see the Lord.

God is Watching

"Are not two sparrows sold for a penny? And not one of them will fall to the ground apart from your Father" Matthew 10:29

"Even before a word is on my tongue, behold, O Lord, you know it altogether" Psalm 139:4

"But the Lord said to Samuel, 'Do not look on his appearance or on the height of his stature, because I have rejected him. For the Lord sees not as man sees: man looks on the outward appearance, but the Lord looks on the heart'" 1 Samuel 16:7

"For the eyes of the Lord run to and fro throughout the whole earth, to give strong support to those whose heart is blameless toward him." 2 Chronicles 16:9

It may seem like it is impossible. How can God be everywhere? How does He know what you are doing and thinking all of the time? As you look at the Scripture, it is evident that God sees more than just us. God created so many wonderful things on this earth. He cares for the planet, the animals, and the people on it.

Throughout the Bible verses, we read so many examples of God's knowing and seeing what is happening all of the time. During the time of the events of the New Testament, the temples of the day (similar to our churches today) practiced offering sacrifices to God. Remember that this was at the time Jesus was on earth and He wanted to change these practices of sacrifices and focus on worshiping God. Around the Temples were areas where people would sell the animals to be sacrificed for offerings. In the first verse above, we see that these sparrows were sold for one penny. In other words, the sparrows were not highly valued. And yet, not even one small bird, that was not valued by mankind, will not fall to the ground without God's knowledge of this. If God pays this much attention to these little birds, imagine how intently He watches and cares for us!

God knows us so well that, as the second passage states, He even knows the words we are going to speak before we are forming the words in our mouths![2] Wow! That is unbelievable! This also means He knows these very words being typed for you before I type them! He provides guidance for a writer communicating to others about God.

The last two verses both indicate that the most important thing that God watches and knows is our heart. He does not judge as mankind judges. He always knows the truth about us even when other people might reject us or be unkind. Know this: **He knows the kindness of your heart**. And as the last verse says, He is looking all over the world for believers because He wants to be sure and support

---

[2] Is Foreknowledge Compatible with Free Will?
https://christianpublishinghouse.co/2018/02/18/is-foreknowledge-compatible-with-free-will/

them. He watches, He cares, He loves, He offers support. We are so thankful that He is watching us.

Animals and Heaven

"So God said "Let the earth bring forth living creatures according to their kinds- livestock and creeping things and beasts of the earth according to their kinds" And so it was. Genesis 1: 24

"Whoever is righteous has regard for the life of their beast..." Proverbs 12:10

"Who teaches us more than the beasts of the earth and makes us wiser than the birds of the heavens?" Job 35:11

"And all flesh shall see the salvation of God" Luke 3:6

"Blessed are those who mourn, for they shall be comforted" Matthew 5:4

"He heals the brokenhearted and binds up their wounds" Psalm 147:3

We are so blessed to have all of the creatures God created for us. He can see in the heart of people and places pets in our lives for our care. As stated in the second verse, people with good hearts take care of their pets and love them as part of the family. In Job, we are reminded that the creations that God gave us, beasts of the earth, and birds, help us to learn. When you were growing up all these years, taking care of your pets has been a way to learn responsibility, but more important than that, it is a way to learn about love and loyalty. These animals are like friends and family. You love them, and they love you right back! When you lose a pet, a dog or cat or other animal, you miss that little creature that God put in your life. But your dog or other pet may have been sick or had a tragic accident. You have taken care of them, loved them, and then you grieve for them when they take their heavenly journey home. These creatures are blessings sent to us so that we may honor the charge that God gave mankind to care for the earth and creatures in it. We care for them and love them while they are with us. Now that your pet is no longer with you, you know your sweet dog is without pain. You can be thankful for the time you shared together.

You will probably need a little time for grieving when you lose a pet. He has been with your family for many years, and it will be tough to move on. But you will. This is possible because, as the last passage states, God will heal you. Know this: **He heals all wounds.** So, remember the good years you had with your pet. Thank God for putting pets in your home for you to love. Say a prayer for your pet that is resting in peace.[3]

---

[3] Are Our Animal Pets Resurrected?
https://christianpublishinghouse.co/2018/04/08/are-our-animal-pets-resurrected/

Terry Overton

Dealing with Tough Days

"Do not be conformed to this world, but be transformed by the renewal of your mind, that by testing you may discern what is the will of God, what is good and acceptable and perfect" Romans 12:2

As we move through each day, we may find it is hard for us to think of anything else except what is right before us. We may have our mind on school, our work, friendships that may not be going well, dating, chores, and interacting with your family. Sometimes we need to stay focused on exactly what we are doing, such as school or homework. Other times, we would do well to get our minds off of these day-to-day matters. We become obsessed with worries on some days. And other days, well everything just seems to go wrong. It is almost like one bad thing is piled up on top of another bad thing and then when you are trying to take a deep breath, another bad thing happens. It is so difficult to think of something pleasant on those days. Our minds just stay focused on the bad things that are happening.

The passage above instructs us not to be conformed or stuck in this world but to transform our thinking to a new frame of mind. What are we supposed to think about? This passage says to think about the will of God. That's a hard one! When things are going badly, we do not want to think that God is making these bad things happen to us on purpose. The good news is, that is not exactly what this verse means. This verse means that it is God's will that you will overcome the bad things or things that "test" you. God wants you to remember the good things, the perfect things, and to use your mind to think about how these tests should be handled in a way that God would like.

How do we do that? How can we be sure that what we think about and do during a difficult time is what God wants us to do? The following verse from Romans tells us to be hopeful and patient, and most important, to constantly pray during this time of trials. You can pray for wisdom to do the right thing, for patience to withstand this trial, and for God's blessings that He might send your way to help you with the trials.

"Rejoice in hope, be patient in tribulation, be constant in prayer" Romans 12:12

Since we can use these difficult times to grow closer to God, we should be joyful that we have this opportunity to try and react as God would like us to do. Jesus said that all of the tests that He has allowed us to go through (not that He has caused them) should be thought of in this way. Know this: **God wants us to lean on Him during these trials, and He rejoices when you come closer to Him and when you ask for His help. He knows you depend on Him.**

"Count it all joy, my brothers, when you meet trials of various kinds" James 1:2

And when you still feel sad, anxious, or weak during these tough days, think about the verse below.

We are not supposed to continue feeling this way, instead we should realize that God will be with you. He will be holding your hand, holding you up when you stumble, and picking you up when you cannot go a step further. With His help, you will make it through tough times and, after the trials, you will be nearer to Him. Rejoice in this!

> *"Have I not commanded you? Be strong and courageous. Do not be frightened, and do not be dismayed, for the Lord your God is with you wherever you go" Joshua 1:9*

Your Personal Faith

"But in your hearts honor Christ the Lord as holy, always being prepared to make a defense to anyone who asks you for a reason for the hope that is in you; yet do it with gentleness and respect" 1 Peter 3:15

"Jesus said to him, 'I am the way, and the truth, and the life. No one comes to the Father except through me.'" John 14:6

Your mind and heart, or soul, are amazing. One study found that we have about 86 billion brain cells and that each one connects to as many as 10,000 others which gives us nearly 1000 trillion connections. Our physical brains are astonishing. But what is more important than the brain is the mind. The mind is your brain functioning as a thinking organ. This is where you understand everything that goes on and where you understand what you read and learn. Part of our brain also processes our feelings, and this is what we may call our soul or "heart" or where we feel things like emotions. This is where our thoughts and feelings about God are kept.

Having your own personal faith is a wonderful way to think about keeping Jesus in your life always. We are instructed to always honor Jesus in our hearts and by keeping Him there; we should be ready to tell others about Him and even defend our belief in Him for those who do not understand. Scripture also tells us that when we defend Jesus, we should do this with kindness. This reflects how Jesus wants us to treat all other people, with kindness.

> *"Be kind to one another, tenderhearted, forgiving one another, as God in Christ forgave you" Ephesians" 4:32*

Know this: **your own personal faith is something that is always in your heart just like the Holy Spirit.** You use your personal faith and the Holy Spirit to understand Bible verses, to think about what Jesus wants you to do, and to pray. Prayer is something else that God believes is very personal. Jesus told us how to pray:

> *"But when you pray, go into your room and shut the door and pray to your Father who is in secret. And your Father who sees in secret will reward you" Matthew 6:6*

Jesus wants us to live our lives with Him inside of our heart and mind. He says that we should use our personal faith every day as we interact with people. We should perform acts of kindness and not expect to receive any reward for doing so because We should not perform kind acts, so others will see us doing so. God knows when we are doing these kind acts. He is watching and will reward us in heaven. These acts of kindness need not be large or noticeable. It can be as simple as helping your parents or brother and sister. It can be as small as doing something for a teacher or friend that they may not notice until later or they may never know who did the kind act.

"Beware of practicing your righteousness before other people in order to be seen by them. for then you will have no reward from your Father who is in heaven" Matthew 6:1

Still Missing My Sweet Dog

"As soon as I heard these words I sat down and wept and mourned for days, and I continued fasting and praying before the God of heaven" Nehemiah 1:4

Hearing bad news can be very upsetting, like when you first heard that your pet was no longer here with your family. The verse above tells us that when Nehemiah heard of the destruction of Jerusalem, he sat down and wept and mourned for days. He even continued his mourning after that and fasted and kept praying. He wanted so badly for Jerusalem to be built back up again and was sad about the loss.

This passage lets us know that mourning is not a quick process. It can take us a while. That is ok. Some people process grief more quickly than others. The feelings about loss may be pretty raw at first. And, since your pet was in your house and yard, and you are still living there, you see those reminders every day. You remember that he would greet you every day when you got home from school, and now he doesn't. It reminds you that he has fallen asleep in death.

What can you do to feel better? First of all, just think about your favorite memories of your pet. If you have pictures of him, you can collect them and put them in a memory book. Or you can draw pictures of how you remember him and name the drawings "Memories of My Dog (or other pet)."

It also helps for you to be with your friends and family that you trust and love. They all know how you feel and will support you through this process. Then, the Bible tells us many times that our next step is to pray and trust God.

"Is anyone among you suffering? Let him pray. Is anyone cheerful? Let him sing praise" James 5:13

Know this: **God will give you the strength to move beyond grief.** All you have to do is ask.

"I can do all things through him who strengthens me" Philippians 4:13

What If My Friends Don't Follow Christ?

"Be imitators of me, as I am of Christ"
1 Corinthians 11:1

"Do your best to present yourself to God as one approved, a worker who has no need to be ashamed, rightly handling the word of truth" 2 Timothy 2:15

Being a child of His Kingdom, you know and understand how wonderful it is to be a Christian. We are excited about our own faith. We become even more excited when we go to church, youth group, read the Bible and celebrate the birth and resurrection of Christ. We could just sing our lungs out sometimes and want to shout from the rooftop!

But what if your friends are not yet in this kingdom? What do they think about you? And can you help them to come to the cross?

Probably it is more difficult to explain what it means to be a Christian than to just live like one. Why? Because, unfortunately, our friends who may not really be believers (yet) may not want to hear about being a believer. They may even feel that we are trying to somehow be better than they are—and we don't want to lose their friendship. But, they already like you. They like you because of the way you interact with them and the way you treat people. As the verses above tell us we should all seek to be imitators of Christ. As you recall from the new testament, as Jesus traveled around during His ministry, He loved all people and treated everyone with kindness. He demonstrated for us how to behave, and others were drawn to Him because of the way He was and the things He said.

The second verse above reminds us that we are to go forward as true workers for God and not be ashamed or afraid of our actions. It also tells us to handle the word of God in a truthful manner. Know this: **we should not hide our faith or apologize for it**. Paul told the Philippians that they should always treat others as more significant than themselves.

"Do nothing from rivalry or conceit, but in humility count others more significant that yourselves" Philippians 2:3.

When your friends realize how you are around them, and they notice how consistently you think of others first, they will one day make a comment or ask you about why. That is when you let them know, "I am a Christian and I try to behave as Jesus would." At that point, you may begin to talk more about your faith and invite them to come with you to youth group or to church.

Helping My Friends Learn More About Christ

"Therefore do not be ashamed of the testimony about our Lord, not of me his prisoner, but share in suffering for the gospel by the power of God" 2 Timothy 1:8

The verses from 2nd Timothy were written by Paul while he was in prison. He felt that teaching others about Jesus was so important that he continued to do so while he was in prison. He sent for his fellow believer, Timothy, to visit him and wanted to be sure that these letters reached Timothy to inform him about the importance of spreading the gospel.

Today, it seems hard for us to know exactly how to talk to our friends to encourage them to grow closer to God and His Son, Jesus. Of course, living by the examples that Jesus showed us is a start, but there may be times when you are puzzled. You may be asking yourself "Should I say something now? Will my talking about Jesus seem too pushy?" Faith is a very sensitive subject because it is buried deeply within us when we believe.

Some people who do not truly yet understand about God, may feel intimidated when we talk about our beliefs. They may wonder if something is wrong with them because they don't understand everything we say. They may also be curious but are embarrassed or hesitant to ask us. So, the question becomes, how to approach the subject? Do you initiate first or wait? Maybe they are too shy to ask.

You can always offer an opportunity for them to ask you a question by saying something like, "If you want to know more about my beliefs, just let me know." And then pray that they will ask you so you can offer information or take them with you to church.

What is the danger if your friends do not want to find out information from a reliable source, like you, your family, a youth group or church? The danger is that they may be pulled in the wrong direction. Paul, while still in prison writing his letters, talked about this:

> *"For the time is coming when people will not endure sound teaching, but having itching ears they will accumulate for themselves teachers to suit their own passions, and will turn away from listening to the truth and wander off into myths"* 2 Timothy 4:3-4

It seems that many people, young and old, fall into this "itchy ear" category of wanting to listen to and believe in things of their own passions rather than from learning the truth. Say a prayer that your friends will want to know more. When they are ready, let them know you are willing to talk all about Jesus. Know this: **God will help you with the words when your friends are ready**.

Am I Ready to Date?

"So flee youthful passions and pursue righteousness, faith, love, and peace, along with those who call on the Lord from a pure heart" 2 Timothy 2:22

This verse is interesting because it was written in a letter from Paul to his younger fellow believer whom he had trained. This book of the Bible contains this letter in which Paul is giving Timothy instructions so that he will continue to go forward and preach even while Paul was in prison. Paul is getting older and wants Timothy to continue spreading the word even though Paul can no longer do so. Paul is telling Timothy not to waste his time on things that don't really matter. He told Timothy to give up youthful ways that are not meaningful. This would be similar to you listening to a teacher, coach, or parent, who wants you to make your life one that is for the good of others. Notice that Paul tells Timothy to give up the foolish things and, instead, to look for righteousness and love as well as peace and faith. He tells Timothy to look for pure hearts that believe in God and His Son.

These words are just as important today. We all want our lives to be significant and to do the things that matter. We all want love. We should strive to be with people who are pure at heart and love God. These are the same types of people we should look for in a dating relationship.

You might wonder if there are any other characteristics that we should look for? The following verse includes so much information about love. Paul is talking about pure love such as the pure unconditional love we have from God. It is a good one to refer to often and ask yourself if the person you are dating has this type of personality.

> *"Love is patient and kind; love does not envy or boast; it is not arrogant or rude. It does not insist on its own way; it is not irritable or resentful; it does not rejoice in wrongdoing, but rejoices with the truth. Love bears all things, believes all things, hopes all things, endures all things" 1 Corinthians 13: 4-7*

If you are talking to someone and think you might want to date that person, go through this list and see if the person shares the values that are important. If not, listen to Paul and give up the youthful passions that are not meaningful for your future. Continue to search for the person with a pure heart. That person is out there looking for someone like you.

Dealing with Peer Pressure

"For what will it profit a man if he gains the whole world and forfeits his soul? Or what shall a man give in return for his soul?" Matthew 16:26

It is so easy to find yourself in the wrong place and the wrong time with the wrong people.[4] It can sneak up on you. Before you know it, four or five of your "friends" have decided to do something that you know is not right. You also know that they may all get in trouble and that they will talk about you if you don't go along. They may make fun of you. They may just decide they will no longer want to hang out with you.

The words in the verse above are from Jesus as He spoke to his disciples. He is asking them an important question. If He happened to drop in on you and your friends when they were scheming to do something that shouldn't be done, Jesus would ask you the very same question. He is asking the disciples, and would ask you, what good is it to win your friends if you have to sin in order to do it? If you participate, you would be sinning. Rather than this small group of mischievous friends talking badly about you if you do not participate, you would have

---

[4] TEENS – Resisting Peer Pressure to Do Wrong
https://christianpublishinghouse.co/2017/08/14/teens-resisting-peer-pressure-to-do-wrong/

the whole school, your parents, and others, talking about the bad things you did with those friends. You would not be right with God because you went along and intentionally did something wrong. Once that happens, do you ever get your good name back? Or, as Jesus said, what could you do to get your soul back? It might not seem like the one thing the friends want to do is very bad, but your troubles would grow if you participate.

The verses below are from Proverbs. This is short, and you could think about them when you are tempted to go along with your friends. The first one says if you go along with the "fools," harm will come to you. So, resist the bad behaviors or sins. Ask God to help you be strong. Change the subject with your friends and ask them to go along with you to do something that won't get you all in trouble. Know this: **in any situation, acting as if Jesus is standing beside you will keep you from trouble.**

"Whoever walks with the wise becomes wise, but the companion of fools will suffer harm" Proverbs 13:20

"My son, if sinners entice you, do not consent" Proverbs 1:10

Deal With Bullying

"Whoever says he is in the light and hates his brother is still in darkness" 1 John 2:9

There should be no bullying ever. You know that, and the people who work at your school know it also. But bullying may still happen. If you have been bullied, or you know someone who is being bullied, it must be reported. Please tell a teacher, a parent, or another adult, as soon as you can.

Why in the world would someone bully another person? It is so unnecessary. The verse above from 1st John tells us why. Individuals who bully are the same people that act as if they are regular good people. They want others to think they would never bother anyone and certainly wouldn't hurt anyone. They want others to believe they are "in the light." But, in truth, acting with hate or aggression shows everyone that the person is still in the dark. They are sinful. They act with evil intentions. And by acting in this way, it is clear they are not following the example set before us by Jesus. They may not know anything about Jesus. So, once you have reported this to an adult at school, do you know what Jesus wants you to do? He wants you to pray for them. That's right. Pray that God can help to remove the evil from their heart. Pray that someone, a parent, an adult, or you and your parents, help bring them to know Christ.

"The Lord is good, a stronghold in the day of trouble; he knows those who take refuge in him" Nahum 1:7

The prophet who wrote the verse above envisioned God as a warrior who would defend him and his people from the country of warriors with whom he fought. In the case of bullying, God will not come down as a warrior to help the person being bullied. But God knows that you or the person being bullied needs help in the day of trouble. He knows those who pray for help. And the way God would fight for you would be to answer prayers asking that the other person finds God. In other words, when the other person finds God, then that person no longer bullies people. It may be hard for you to help this other person, but someone else could. Know this: **God wants you to pray for those who do not know about Him.** Ask your parents or a teacher how this person can get the help he or she needs. Then pray the help will work.[5]

---

[5] TEENS – How Do I Deal With Bullies?
https://christianpublishinghouse.co/2017/08/29/teens-how-do-i-deal-with-bullies/

Forgiving Others

"Then Peter came up and said to him, 'Lord, how often will my brother sin against me, and I forgive him? As many as seven times?' and Jesus said to him, 'I do not say to you seven times, but seventy times seven'" Matthew 18: 21-22

Forgiveness may seem impossible for us sometimes. It is especially hard to do when you feel you have been wronged and you want the other person to get punished. You may feel so much anger at the person that you cannot imagine forgiving the person. But Jesus was serious about this. When Peter asked him, Jesus said that Peter was not expected to forgive the person seven times but a whopping 490 times!

Why was forgiveness so important to Jesus when He was here on earth? He knew he was here to die for us so that we would be forgiven. Forgiveness was the reason he came to earth and the reason He was sacrificed. So, He was very serious.

Jesus also told us that we should forgive others just like we would be forgiven. In fact, He said if we want forgiveness, we also must forgive.

"For if you forgive others their trespasses, your heavenly Father will also forgive you, but if you do not forgive others

their trespasses, neither will your Father forgive your trespasses" Matthew 6: 14-15

If you have difficulty with forgiveness after reading these verses, it may help you to remember that the person that did the action against you was doing this out of weakness. The person was tempted and could not resist. The action indicates that the person could not resist the temptation. This is what you are forgiving. Know this: **you are forgiving their weakness, just as you have weaknesses and must be forgiven**. And, after you have forgiven the person, say a prayer and ask for you and the other person have more strength and resist weakness.

Forgiving Yourself

"If we confess our sins, he is faithful and just to forgive us our sins and to cleanse us from all unrighteousness" 1 John 1:9

Although it may be difficult to forgive others who did something wrong, you can pray about it, and God will help you to forgive the other person for their weakness. But have you ever thought about how hard it is to forgive yourself? As the verse says above, once we confess, we are cleansed from all of the acts that we did in a moment of weakness. That is easier to say than to do.

Have you ever done something, either because of bad judgment, a mistake, or you just kind of weren't thinking seriously about what you were doing? And then, it turns out to be horrible for you and perhaps another person? And even though you might have asked for forgiveness from the other person and from God, you just can't stop "beating yourself up" about the mistake you made? You might just keep reliving the nightmare in your head over and over and asking, "How could I have done something so stupid?"

When you continue to give yourself a hard time about a mistake you made, you are punishing yourself needlessly. Do you know why? If you are punishing yourself, you have now assumed that you are the judge because you decide if you have been punished enough.

Judgement and forgiveness are only up to God. Once you asked for forgiveness, you can let the mistake go. You are saved by grace. Know this: **You are forgiven by God's grace therefore, you cannot continue to punish yourself.** Learn from the mistake but let it go, you have received God's grace.

> *For by grace you have been saved through faith. And this is not your own doing; it is the gift of God..." Ephesians 2:8-9*

So, what do you do next? Let the negative self-punishing thoughts go and think thoughts about pleasant things. This is what God wants us to do. In the New Testament, Paul wrote a letter to the Philippians and, in that letter, he instructed believers that they should always be thinking good thoughts.

> *"Finally, brothers, whatever is true, whatever is honorable, whatever is just, whatever is pure, whatever is lovely, whatever is commendable, if there is any excellence, if there is anything worthy of praise, think about these things" Philippians 4:8*

Terry Overton

Being Thankful for People in Your Life Who Challenge You

> *"For it is not an enemy who taunts me-then I could bear it; it is not an adversary who deals insolently with me-then I could hide from him. But it is you, a man, my equal, my companion, my familiar friend"* Psalm 55:12-13

> *"Do you see a man who is wise in his own eyes? There is more hope for a fool than for him"* Proverbs 26:12

> *"Be strong and courageous. Do not fear or be in dread of them, for it is the Lord your God who goes with you. He will not leave you or forsake you"* Deuteronomy 31:6

Some of your friends, teachers, or others that you see every day can be very challenging people. The first verse above says that it is easier to have an enemy bother you than a friend. If it was an enemy, you could get away from that person and not interact with them anymore. But people that you see each day can challenge you for many reasons. A friend or teacher may appear as a "know it all." This type of person may speak to others in a way that makes everyone else seem small, dumb, or not important. As the second verse says, these people may be beyond hope! You might also notice the people who seem to know everything do not have many friends because others may avoid them! But sometimes they are right about many things, and you may end up thanking them for a correct response or for the help they provide you. Others may make you feel nervous, anxious, or afraid. One example is a very strict teacher that keeps you on your toes but from whom you learned more than you did from other teachers. Another type of difficult person might be someone who has an unpredictable mouth. They might embarrass you or say something that causes unrest among friends. These mouthy people may not have many friends either and, in fact, you might be their only friend. Challenging people provide you with an opportunity to improve your people skills. If you can figure them out, you will actually be a great employee in the future because you would have learned how to get along with everyone! This also helps you to learn about compromise which will be important in marriage later.

The verse below is one that can be applied to many situations and is a great one for being thankful for difficult people. These are just temporary trials. God is always there to provide you with guidance when you ask Him. Learning to get along with all people in the manner Jesus would expect will actually be rewarded in the future. Know this: **God put these people in your path so that you can learn these lessons about people.** Thank Him for these opportunities!

"In this you rejoice, though now for a little while, if necessary, you have been grieved by various trials, so that the tested

genuineness of your faith-more precious than gold that perishes though it is tested by fire-may be found to result in praise and glory and honor at the revelation of Jesus Christ" 1 Peter 1:6-7

Difficult Times in Dating

"Then God said, it is not good that the man should be alone; I will make him a helper fit for him" Genesis 2:18

When God created man, He knew that he would need a companion. And so, here we are now. Men and women, boys and girls. In truth, God didn't exactly give Adam and Eve a roadmap. He simply told them there was one thing they should not do…and you know how that story ended! So, the best way to work in a dating partnership and, later marriage, is a mystery. But it can be a wonderful mystery! It can be so exciting and loving. But dating as a teen can be just outright confusing!

It is always exciting to begin dating a new person. It is fun to get to know that person, what they like to do, the music they like, and places they like to go. When you spend more time with a person you are dating; you have opportunities for long conversations and fun experiences. But, sometimes tricky situations happen. These situations can be awkward moments when you are talking about your friends and realize that the other person doesn't get along with one of your friends. It can be awkward when you say something that you think might be funny but the person you are dating takes it as an insult or misunderstands the meaning. There can be even more serious problems when you are dating. Maybe the other person seems to feel more serious about the relationship than you do. Maybe the other person says or does something that makes you uncomfortable. Or, maybe you feel more strongly about the person than they seem to feel for you. How do you handle these types of situations?

"Trust in the Lord with all your heart, and do not lean on your own understanding. In all your ways acknowledge him, and he will make straight your paths" Proverbs 3:5-6

You can consult the Scriptures, such as the one above, that tells you to trust God with all your heart and to try not to figure everything out on your own. Just trust that the way God wants you to handle all other situations is the same way you would handle dating situations. Rely on God to keep a straight path. And also remember that God granted you parents and other adults in your life to help instruct you in all things, including dating. If something just does not feel right to you, trust your heart. Pay careful attention to your feelings. If you feel uneasy about something, there is a reason for it. God is helping you at that point to listen to the godliness in your heart. You know the right thing to do.

"But as for you, continue in what you have learned and have firmly believed, knowing from whom you learned it" 2 Timothy 3:14

Know this: **God and your parents are always looking out for you; ask them difficult questions and follow their answers.** Pray. Be thankful for your loving guidance from your family.

Praising God (Give God the Glory)

"And whatever you do, in word or deed, do everything in the name of the Lord Jesus, giving thanks to God the Father through him" Colossians 3:17

The verse above is pretty straightforward. But it is helpful to understand the context of these words in the Bible. You might remember that Paul was selected by God to spread the good news of Jesus. But he was not a believer at first. In fact, he was against Christianity. But, once he became a believer, he wrote many letters to different congregations in order to explain the teachings of Jesus. As a matter of fact, Paul wrote 12 of the 66 books in the Bible! Before he wrote the verse above to the congregation, he told them that they were to live their new life in Christ, following righteousness, resisting sin, and to be very careful of false teachings. He wanted to be sure that the people of this congregation knew that all of their blessings were because of the love and the glory of God, no matter what they heard from false teachers.

Thinking about your life and world today, you have so many blessings and opportunities and, just like the Colossians, everything you have is because of God's love. But when you have worked really hard to achieve something, it is easy to understand that you feel that you have put forth the effort and the work and you should get some of the credit. That is true. You did put forth the effort. You did the hard work. But your skills, your energy, your ability, your mind, are all gifts from God. So, when you have a wonderful outcome, win a swim meet, a band contest, make an excellent grade on an assignment, congratulate yourself and thank God for giving you your abilities to be successful. Know this: **you put forth the work, and God gave you the ability to do so!**

"But thanks be to God, who gives us the victory through our Lord Jesus Christ" 1 Corinthians 15:57

Once the awards are given, and you have offered thanks to God, remember to praise Him and let others know how grateful you are to God and to your teammates, friends, and others, for their help.

"I will praise the name of God with a song; I will magnify him with thanksgiving" Psalm 69:30

Turn to God in Times of Pain and Rejoice

"For God called you to do good, even if it means suffering, just as Christ suffered for you. He is your example and you must follow in his steps" 1 Peter 2:21

No matter what anyone tells you, life is full of ups and downs. You will have wondrous days, and you will have days when you wonder why you even got out of bed. Our bad days can include feelings of stress, anxiety, and pain. We can have physical symptoms of pain and stress, or we can experience mental or psychological pain. During these times, it is hard to remember that we have a new life in Christ and that our lives are so joyful. When we stop for a moment and remember we are believers, the verse above makes so much sense. We are all trying to do good, just as we were called to do. Nevertheless, we will have pain and suffering. But, so did Jesus. He became human so that He could relate to our troubles and feelings and also so that we would know that He understands our suffering. He has walked these same steps of pain and even anxiety. Imagine—He knew He was going to suffer for us yet He continued to love people and help everyone who requested His help, and He did so with a glad heart.

"And after you have suffered a little while, the God of all grace, who has called you to his eternal glory in Christ, will

himself restore, confirm, strength, and establish you" 1 Peter 5:10

In this verse, we are reminded that, after our suffering, we will be stronger. We are children of the King. We will be restored and strengthened. What should we do when we are in the middle of pain? We simply ask for God's help no matter what is going on in our lives. Know this: **Jesus suffered, and he understands our pain and can give us strength.** When our pain brings us nearer to God, we feel better, and He rejoices in our faith. God has blessed you with His grace and will make you stronger.

"Have I not commanded you? Be strong and courageous. Do not be frightened, and do not be dismayed, for the Lord your God is with you wherever you go" Joshua 1:9

Dealing with Anger

We can become angry very quickly. Sometimes we might have a good reason to get angry. Someone said something that was uncalled for, hurt us, insulted us, or did something against us. Other times, a person's behavior might be misinterpreted. Maybe they thought they were saying something funny and we misunderstood. Maybe they were pulling a prank but it upset us. Maybe they even conspired with other people to do something ugly to us. Maybe they lied to us. We can become angry. What did God do when He was angry?

> *"For my names' sake I defer my anger,*
> *for the sake of my praise I restrain it for you,*
> *that I may not cut you off" Isaiah 48:9*

In this Old Testament Verse, God is expressing His anger toward Israel. He then says, even though He is angry with them, He is not going to show His anger. He says He is holding back anger, so He will not "cut off" or destroy Israel. In this example, we see God demonstrating for us what we are to do with anger. Defer from action.

"*Be angry and do not sin, do not let the sun go down on your anger and give no opportunity to the devil*" Ephesians 4:26-27

In Paul's letter of instructions to the Ephesians, he offers plenty of advice about how the congregation should handle their anger. He first tells them to take care of anger quickly. We should not harbor anger. One of the things we might do in a moment of weakness is let the anger fly out of our mouths! Yikes! Paul even addresses that!

> *"Let no corrupting talk come out of your mouths, but only such as is good for building up, as fits the occasion, that it may give grace to all who hear" Ephesians 4:29*

He instructed the congregation to use their mouths for only good comments. Our parents used to tell us the same thing: If you can't say something nice, don't say anything! But Paul continues by telling us, just as Jesus did, that when we feel anger, we have to get rid of all of that evil behavior and be kind to each other.

> *"Get rid of all bitterness, rage, anger, harsh words, and slander, as well as all types of evil behavior. Instead, be kind to each other, tenderhearted, forgiving one another, just as God through Christ has forgiven you" Ephesians 4:31-32*

Know this: We are to forgive those who make us angry. It may be difficult to do right away. So, take a deep breath, defer from acting right away as God did with Israel, and then think about how you will be able to forgive the person for their weakness. Chances are, if you make the first step to making peace with those who made you angry, they will also take steps to resolve the issue.[6]

---

[6] Let All Wrath and Anger Be Put Away From Us

God's Voice

"In the beginning was the Word, and the Word was with God, and the Word was God" John 1:1

Everything began with God. God, being too big for us to truly comprehend, communicated with mankind through divine knowledge. This knowledge was written, over thousands of years, in the books, we now know as the Bible. So, the voice of God is heard in many ways. The first was through the word of God which is the Bible. The knowledge that is contained in the Bible is the living word of God.

"But he answered, 'It is written, 'Man shall not live by bread alone, but by every word that comes from the mouth of God'"
Matthew 4:4

When Jesus was in the desert before He began his ministry, He was tempted by the devil who knew that Jesus was hungry. Jesus, being perfect and sinless, did not listen to the devil who wanted Him to turn stones into bread. Jesus told the devil that it was not only bread that man needs to survive but the words of God. Jesus is telling the devil, and us, how important the words from God are in our lives.

We all know the Bible is the living word of God, but some people who read it just don't seem to

---

https://christianpublishinghouse.co/2016/10/24/let-all-wrath-and-anger-be-put-away-from-us/

understand it at all. They may be reading it as they would any other story or book. But for those who are believers in God, we understand the meanings of the written words from God. The reason we can understand these words is that the Holy Spirit is guiding us through the Spirit inspired word, as we buy out the time from less important things, to do personal Bible study. In the verse below, Jesus was speaking to the people who did not believe in Him. He knew that they did not have the Spirit within them to understand what he was telling them.

"Whoever is of God hears the words of God. The reason why you do not hear them is that you are not from God" John 8:47

At another time, Jesus was being questioned once again by a crowd who did not believe in Him. Again, He stated that those who believe can understand what He was saying.

"My sheep hear my Voice, and I know them, and they follow me" John 10:27

For us today, to hear the word of God, we begin by reading the word of God. Since we are able to understand the meanings, we are able to hear God's voice. He is speaking to us through the written word. As a believer, once you become familiar with the words of God, you can hear his voice even when you are not reading the Bible at that very moment. The Holy Spirit keeps those meanings in your heart and mind. This is why you might be able to tell exactly what God wants you to do in so many situations. Know this: **God's voice is within those who have**

accepted Jesus in their hearts and remember the words of God in their minds. Keep reading. Keep studying the words and the voice will be readily available to you.

Intentional Giving

"And he sat down opposite the treasure and watched the people putting money into the offering box. Many rich people put in large sums. And a poor widow came and put in two small copper coins, which make a penny. And he called his disciples to him and said to them, 'Truly, I say to you, this poor widow has put in more than all those who are contributing to the offering box. For they all contributed out of their abundance, but she out of her poverty has put in everything she had, all she had to live on." Mark 12:41-44

You may feel that you have nothing to give to other people. As the verse above tells us, Jesus does not believe the amount of what you give is important. He tells us that it is your willingness to give whatever you have. So, if you do not have a lot of money to donate to something you feel strongly about, that is ok. You can donate what you have. It is proportional in the verse above. Jesus noticed that the widow gave a penny but that was more meaningful than what all of the other people had given. So, it is not the amount, it is the heart of giving that is important.

"If a brother or sister is poorly clothed and lacking in daily food, and one of you says to them, 'Go in peace, be warmed and

filled, without giving them the things needed for the body, what good is that?" James 2:15-16

"In all things I have shown you that by working hard in this way we must help the weak and remember the words of the Lord Jesus, how he himself said, 'It is more blessed to give than to receive," Acts 20:35

In these verses, we see that giving should include meeting the needs of people who are poor, or who need the very basic things that all humans need, should be a part of our giving. We should not be content just to be nice to them and think that is enough. If others are suffering, we should help them. And, any type of giving to those in need is actually better for the giver! So, we rejoice that we are able to help others. It will actually feel better to us than when we receive a gift. **Know this: giving from the heart is better than anything you can receive.**

One of the most important instructions we are given by Jesus is not to make a big deal out of our giving. We are to keep it to ourselves. In Matthew, Jesus said that some people like to sound a trumpet to announce their giving. They are giving just to get attention for it. It is not giving from the heart. Jesus said that even our left hand should not know what our right hand is doing! Now that is a secret!

"But when you give to the needy, do not let your left hand know what your right hand is doing, so that your giving may be in

secret. And your Father who sees in secret will reward you." Matthew 6: 3-4

Responsibility

"For each will have to bear his own load" Galatians 6:5

Responsibility is a topic that sometimes makes us shrug our shoulders and say, "Uh oh, here we go. Another lecture." We might think responsibility is all our parents and teachers talk about! We hear the word responsibility used about homework, school work, work for other people if we have a job, work around the house such as cleaning and laundry. In fact, responsibility can be a pretty boring word.

And then we look at what the Bible has to say about that word. Did you know that the verse above was written by Paul to the congregation in Galatia because he was concerned about this congregation? The members of this congregation, who had only recently become followers of Christ, were being told to work hard for the church. Paul told them not to brag about their work but to judge for themselves if their work was good enough since everyone would need to bear their own responsibility. All of the members were to work together and not worry about who was better.

"He who plants and he who waters are one, and each will receive his wages according to his labor" 1 Corinthians 3:8

It is interesting that this message above was written by Paul to another congregation, the Corinthians, who were concerned about who was doing what. Who is working harder? Who will receive the glory? He told the congregation that their work is for God and that He will be the one to pay the reward. He reminds us that we are all working for the same church and the same purpose.

> "Having gifts that differ according to the grace given to us, let us use them; if prophecy, in proportion to our faith; if service, in our serving; the one who teaches, in his teaching; the one who exhorts, in his exhortation; the one who contributes, in generosity; the one who leads, with zeal, the one who does acts of mercy, with cheerfulness." Romans 12:6-8

In his letter to the Roman believers, Paul reminds us all, that in addition to each of us pulling our own weight, we are to do so cheerfully. He tells us something very important here. We each have different talents. We should all work equally hard, and cheerfully, but we might be doing different things. Know this: **God says it is our responsibility to work hard, using our talents and gifts, and to do so cheerfully.** Paul told his believers that we are not to worry about who is better, who works the hardest, but instead we are to all be cheerful carrying out our own responsibilities.

As it turns out, the word responsibility is pretty important! We are each to carry our own load cheerfully.

Commitment

"Jesus said to him, 'No one who puts his hand to the plow and looks back is fit for the kingdom of God'" Luke 9:62

Over the years, as you have been growing up, you have heard your parents tell you about commitment. Perhaps you told someone you would babysit, but then a friend called with a fun invitation, and you wanted to get out of the babysitting job. Perhaps you joined a sports team and then decided you didn't like practicing so many days a week. But your parents and coach said, "You already made the commitment." And, of course, there is always the commitment to school, your grades, and your future.

In Luke's verse above, he has told us the story about Jesus talking to new believers. Jesus was informing these new believers that if they say they want to become part of His kingdom, there is no looking back. Once you make the commitment, you must stick to it. You have to be "all in" if you are looking to the final reward.

Committing to God and believing in Jesus benefits us while we are here on earth as well. As the verses say below, when you commit to God and pray to Him, He will answer. It may not be in a way you would expect, but the answer will come. And whatever your works may be, when you are doing these works to glorify God, then things will work out as they should.

"Commit your way to the Lord; trust in him, and he will act," Psalm 37:5

"Commit your work to the Lord, and your plans will be established," Proverbs 16:3

But what about commitments to each other? It is understandable that committing to God will benefit Christians as they act help people and the church. But does the Bible also suggest that we should keep the commitments we make to each other? Making a commitment to do something is making a promise. The person to whom you made the promise is expecting that you made the commitment with your whole heart that you would do whatever you promised. This is serious to Christians. The verses below from the New and Old Testament tell us that, if we are following God as true believers, we need to consider our promises with seriousness. And, once we make a commitment, we do as we promised with love.

"Therefore, having put away falsehood, let each one of you speak the truth with his neighbor, for we are members of one another," Ephesians 4:25

"Lying lips are an abomination to the Lord, but those who act faithfully are his delight," Proverbs 12:22

Know this: **A commitment to Jesus and the church includes being truthful to God and each other.** If you have doubts about commitments, refer to these verses. Pray. And act with your heart.

God as the Son

"And the Word became flesh and dwelt among us, and we have seen his glory, glory as of the only Son from the Father, full of grace and truth" John 1:14

"I and the Father are one" John 10:30

Understanding that God is three-in-one is a complex concept. This was difficult for people to understand when Jesus walked on earth. In fact, the Jewish people at the time, and more specifically the priests of the temples, did not understand it. They just couldn't get their brains wrapped around the fact that God's presence was among them in the form of a human. This lack of understanding led to the eventual crucifixion. In order to get the initial group of followers to understand what was happening, in the verses below from the book of Mark, God announced to the people that Jesus was indeed His Son when He was baptized by John.

"And a voice came from heaven, 'You are my beloved Son, with you I am well pleased'" Mark 1:11

Jesus was quick to let His followers know that His power was from His Father. Jesus often spoke of His Father in Heaven and the Holy Spirit. Jesus came to live among people of the earth so that He could show us how to live our lives. But His Father knew that in order for us to believe that Jesus was from

God, we had to know that Jesus was sinless, like His Father, and suffered pain like us. This is why it was important for Him to be here on earth and then to be sacrificed for our sins. But the only way we can ever make it to the Kingdom is through our belief in Jesus.

> *"So Jesus said to them. "Truly, truly, I say to you, the Son can do nothing of his own accord, but only what he sees the Father doing. For whatever the Father does, that the Son does likewise"' John 5:19*

> *"So Jesus said to them, 'When you have lifted up the Son of Man, then you will know that I am he, and that I do nothing on my own authority, but speak just as the Father taught me'" John 8:28*

Know this: **God the Father sent His Son so we might understand our own path to heaven.** The Holy Spirit helps us to understand this complex relationship between God the Father and His Son.

God as the Father

"Before the mountains were brought forth, or even you had formed the earth and the world, from everlasting to everlasting, you are God" Psalm 90: 2

God. What an awesome word. How do you think about the concept of God? God created everything and has been in existence always and always will be. That is an amazing thought. Imagine, creating everything! Just look outside your window at the world and think about the mind of God being able to create everything you see outside! It is just too much to think about! How complex His mind must be! As the verse above from Psalm reminds us, He was here before anything and always will remain.

"One God and Father of all, who is over all and through all and in all" Ephesians 4:6

Not only does God the Father of everything have an unimaginable mind, He has all the strength and power of everything. He causes the elements to provide us weather, water, earth, sun, wind, and even more amazing, the power within our own hearts and minds. You can always ask God the Father for help, strength, courage, love, and hope. He is always listening and knows how to provide what we need.

*"But now, O Lord, you are our Father;
we are the clay, and you are our potter; we
are all the work of your hand" Isaiah 64:8*

Our heavenly Father shapes us into the best person we can be when we depend on Him. When you think of Him before you do or say things, He will guide you. He provides you with the experience, the learning, and the tests you need to live more like He expects. The tests of life can be difficult, but we know these are provided to us to make us better people.

But the most amazing thing God has ever done for us was to give us His Son. He knew that humans cannot live perfect lives. He loves us so much that He wanted to help us out when we manage to get ourselves into trouble. God the Father gave us God the Son.

*"For God so loved the world, that he
gave his only Son, that whoever believes in
him should not perish but have eternal life"
John 3:16.*

Know this: **God the Father, creator of everything, provided us with the gift of eternal life by sacrificing His only Son for us.** This is our greatest gift and is the most love we will receive in our lifetime. Thank Him every day.

God as the Holy Spirit

"For all who are led by the Spirit of God are the sons of God" Romans 8:14

Understanding the Holy Spirit, or the Spirit of God, may be difficult. Sometimes we think about a spirit like a ghost or a burst of wind that just blows by. But the Holy Spirit is nothing like that. All believers are touched by the Spirit of God. As the verse states above, we are led by the Spirit. For believers, the Spirit is so real that it can be felt inside. It is what we hear when we read Scripture. The Spirit is in our minds when we ask God for guidance. The Spirit fills your heart with love for others. The Spirit is within us all of the time.

The brothers immediately sent Paul and Silas away by night to Berea, and when they arrived they went into the Jewish synagogue. Now these Jews were more noble than those in Thessalonica; they received the word with all eagerness, examining the Scriptures daily to see if these things were so. Acts 17:10-11

Unlike the natural person, the Bereans accepted, received, or welcomed the Word of God eagerly. Paul said the Thessalonians "received [*dechomai*] the word in much affliction, with the joy of the Holy Spirit." (1 Thess. 1:6) At the beginning of a person's introduction to the good news, he will take in the knowledge of the Scriptures (1 Tim. 2:3-4), which if his heart is receptive, he will begin to apply them in his life, taking off the old person and putting on the new person. (Eph. 4:22-24) Seeing how the Scriptures have begun to alter his life, he will start to have a genuine faith in the things he has learned (Heb. 11:6), repenting of his sins. (Acts 17:30-31) He will turn around his life, and his sins will be blotted out. (Acts 3:19) At some point, he will go to God in prayer, telling the Father that he is dedicating his life to him, to carry out his will and purposes. (Matt. 16:24; 22:37) This regeneration is the Holy Spirit working in his life, giving him a new nature, placing him on the path to salvation. 2 Corinthians 5:17.

The Holy Spirit will guide us into and through the truth, by way of our working on behalf of our prayers to have the correct understanding. Our working in harmony with the Holy Spirit means that we buy out the time for a personal study program, not to mention the time to prepare properly and carefully for our Christian meetings. In these studies, do not expect that the Holy Spirit is going to give us some flash of understanding miraculously, but rather understanding will come to us as we set aside our personal biases, worldviews, human imperfections, presuppositions, preunderstanding, opening our mental disposition to the Spirit's leading as we study.

The Holy Spirit works only through the Word in the conversion of sinners. In other words, the Spirit acting through the Word of God can accomplish everything claimed to be affected by a personal indwelling of the Spirit. The Holy Spirit transforms a person, empowering him through the Word of God, to put on the "new person" required of true

Christians, "So, as those who have been chosen of God, holy and beloved, put on a heart of compassion, kindness, humility, gentleness and patience." – Colossians 3:12.

> *"And I will ask the Father, and he will give you another Helper, to be with you forever, even the Spirit of truth, whom the world cannot receive, because it neither sees him nor knows him. You know him, for he dwells with you and will be in you"* John 14:16-17

The Spirit helps us to know right from wrong. It knows the truth about Jesus and God and keeps them in your heart and mind. The verse below tells us that the Spirit, given to us by God, guides us and it comes from God.

> *"When the Spirit of truth comes, he will guide you into all truth, for he will not speak on his own authority, but whatever he hears he will speak, and he will declare to you the things that are to come"* John 16:13

Know this: **The Holy Spirit, given from the Father at the request of the Son, is always with you.** Listen to this wonderful resource from God who loves you. The Spirit will guide you and help you.[7]

---

[7] The Holy Spirit and Jesus (http://tiny.cc/sibwqy)
The Holy Spirit and the Apostles (http://tiny.cc/vgbwqy)
The Holy Spirit in the First Century and Today (http://tiny.cc/pabwqy)
The Holy Spirit and the Apostolic Church (http://tiny.cc/3fbwqy)

Making Choices

"Then you will understand righteousness and justice and equity, every good path, for wisdom will come into your heart, and knowledge will be pleasant to your soul; discretion will watch over you, understanding will guard you, delivering you from the way of evil..." Proverbs 2: 9-12

You are faced with choices every day. Some are easy, and you do not even have to think before you answer. Do you want eggs or cereal? Do you need a coat to go outside? But other choices are more complicated, and you find yourself thinking before you make the decision. Do you say yes to the invitation to a party at a friend's house when you do not know that friend very well? Do you say yes to the party invitation when you know the parents will not be there? Do you decide to go to college or to get a job and help out your family?

The Holy Spirit and the World (http://tiny.cc/ffbwqy)
The Work of the Holy Spirit (http://tiny.cc/sjbwqy)
How Are We to Understand the Indwelling of the Holy Spirit? (http://tiny.cc/1mbwqy)
How Do We Receive the Holy Spirit Today? (http://tiny.cc/lel7qy)
Are Answers to Our Prayerful Requests Absolutely Guaranteed? (http://tiny.cc/6yk7qy)
Is Foreknowledge Compatible with Free Will? (http://tiny.cc/1i1isy)

The verse above from Proverbs is taken from a section in which a father is giving his son advice. The main point of this advice is that if the son is grounded in wisdom, by having knowledge of what God expects, then he will be able to make the correct decision. The knowledge about what God wants us to do will help us to make the right choice because we will understand discretion or making fine distinctions between one choice and another. Sometimes when these choices are very close, we can make a list of pros and cons, and this will help us to see what God would expect of us. The father also told his son that having knowledge would protect him from making the wrong choice which would be an evil choice.

"for I will give you a mouth and wisdom, which none of your adversaries will be able to withstand or contradict" Luke 21:15

The verse above is one in which Jesus was telling His disciples that they would be taken prisoner, persecuted, and their lives would be in danger, but not to worry! Why? Because God would provide them with the knowledge, they would need. Their enemies would not be able to come up with any answers when the disciples spoke. Now if Jesus himself talked about using the wisdom of God to respond to difficult situations, then this same wisdom is pretty important for you, too.

"But we impart a secret and hidden wisdom of God, which God decreed before the ages for our glory" 1 Corinthians 2:7

In this letter that Paul wrote to the believers in Corinth, he said that believers have a secret wisdom that has been known and decreed by God since the beginning. That secret knowledge is from the Holy Spirit. For Christians, we know that the Holy Spirit is already in us. That is the voice you reason with in your own mind that will guide you to make the choice that God wants you to make. Know this: **The Holy Spirit will guide you to make the choices that Jesus would make.** Listen to the knowledge. Read about it. Pray for guidance when the decisions are difficult. If the wrong choice is made, it could impact the rest of your life. It is what is called a "life decision." In other words, from that day forward, everything would change for the worse if you make the wrong decision. Depend on your secret knowledge.

Controlling Your Emotions

"Be not quick in your spirit to become angry, for anger lodges in the hearts of fools" Ecclesiastes 7:9

"And which of you by being anxious can add a single hour to his span of life?" Matthew 6:27

"My soul is bereft of peace; I have forgotten what happiness is" Lamentations 3:17

Our minds are capable of so many emotions. Sometimes it is difficult to be certain that you are reacting in the correct way and with the correct amount of a specific emotion. When you have a frustrating experience with a friend, your emotions can range from disappointment to anxiety, to sadness, and even anger. Here is an example of your changing emotions: You might have expected your friend to do or say something different than he or she did, so you can feel disappointed. And maybe the more you think about it, you start to wonder if they are mad at you, so you feel anxiety. And then you move on from anxiety to sadness thinking you might lose a friend. But maybe you also think that whatever happened was uncalled for, so you become angry! Does any of this sound familiar?

The verses above tell us that reacting with anger is not what those who are wise in the word of God should do. To react angrily is foolish and not a good use of our hearts and minds. Worrying also is useless. When we worry, we are spending time and energy that could be used productively. Instead of worrying, we could be following the examples set for us by Jesus. We could speak kindly with the person who has upset us and really listen with our hearts rather than reacting. And remember that when our hearts and minds are filled with the emotions of anger, anxiety, and sadness all of the time, we forget about happiness. In the verse below, we are told that, when we face a serious situation or challenge, we are to reason it out and try to understand it rather than take it too lightly. In other words, if the situation is serious, we should not be silly. It is better to be serious, understand any wrongdoing or true crisis, and then we will be more in touch with our hearts. This verse is telling us it is important to know the difference in all of our emotions.

"Sorrow is better than laughter, for by sadness of face the heart is made glad" Ecclesiastes 7:3

When you know Christ and the wisdom in the Bible, you can rely on this wisdom when you are placed in an emotional situation. Those with this wisdom know they should take their time, not react quickly, look to the Bible for wisdom, and pray for guidance.

"You make known to me the path of life; in your presence there is fullness of joy; at your right hand are pleasures forevermore" Psalm 16:11

Know this: **Our emotions are a gift from God, and our wisdom of Him and His Son will guide us in how to use these emotions.**

Holiness and Happiness

"Do not think that I have come to abolish the Law or the Prophets; I have not come to abolish them but to fulfil them."
Matthew 5:17

Did you know Jesus was a troublemaker? During his three-year ministry, He was questioned by the Jewish priests numerous times. The priests accused Him of breaking their laws of holiness and disobeying the Prophets of the Old Testament. The priests insisted that Jesus was not holy because He did things, like heal people on the Sabbath, that went against their laws. Jesus got into trouble because He told the priests that they were not keeping the laws as God had intended them. God's purpose for holiness was for us to try to live our lives as Jesus did. Jesus told the priests that holiness was not about keeping rituals. Holiness means living your life by loving others as Jesus did, keeping the commandments, and seeking forgiveness when you sin. Since God knew that humans could not keep from sinning, although we try, His Son would be able to pay for all of our sins. God knew that Jesus would be able to give everlasting life for those who believe Him. Jesus came to earth just to be sacrificed for us.

"As obedient children, do not be conformed to the passions of your former ignorance, but as he who called you is holy, you also be holy in all your conduct, since it

is written, "You shall be holy, for I am holy"
1 Peter 1:14-16

In the verse above, we are told that as children, we did things because we did not know better. We did these things because we were excited and were not yet able to think about the consequences of our own actions. But as we became Christians, we are now children of the King. We are now to try for holiness by living our lives as Jesus did when He was among mankind. This type of holiness is different than the holiness of the priests during the time of Jesus. As the verse below tells us, if we get along with everyone, we have peace because we love God and others as Jesus instructed, then we are living in holiness.

"Strive for peace with everyone, and for the holiness without which no one will see the Lord" Hebrews," 12:14

But can we really be happy if we are holy? This can be confusing because even today some people think being holy is the same as being religious. Being religious can mean acting as the priests did—just keeping rituals but not really believing in what Jesus taught. In truth, those who are believers and live as much like Jesus as possible will also be happy. This is what God wants us to do in order to be happy. Know this: **When we live like Jesus, the Spirit inspired Word of God is in our hearts, and we will obey the Word; doing what we know as right and wrong, and we will find happiness in Jesus.**

"I perceived that there is nothing better for them than to be joyful and to do good as long as they live;" Ecclesiastes 3:12

"I delight in your will, O my God; your law is within my heart" Psalm 40:8

Keeping Your Integrity

"Pray for us, for we are sure that we have a clear conscience, desiring to act honorably in all things" Hebrews 13:18

If you look up the word "integrity" in the dictionary, the definitions focus on the concept of a moral code. What exactly does that mean? When we have a code of good behavior that we follow, we have a moral code. This idea of integrity is mentioned many times in the Old and New Testaments. In the first verse above, the early teachers of the good news about Christ and the new church are asking that others pray that the group of workers for Christ are honorable in all things. In the Old Testament, we are told that integrity is more important than having money. Here, it states that it is better to be poor as long as you have a good moral code and live your life trying to keep the word of God.

"Better is a poor man who walks in his integrity than a rich man who is crooked in his ways" Proverbs 28:6

The verse below was written by Paul to the congregation in Corinth. He reminds the congregation that the focus should be not only on righteous to God but also how we treat people. This is another example of pointing out to the people, that being righteous and holy is not just about living within the laws of the church of that time, but also integrity is important in dealing with others. This ties in with the commandment given by Christ to love one another.

"We aim at what is honorable not only in the Lord's sight but also in the sight of man" 2 Corinthians 8:21

The verse from Luke states this more specifically by telling us always to treat others how we want to be treated. So, when you think about it, in order to have a life of integrity, you must always be thinking about other people and treating them as you would want to be treated. Of course, you would not steal from anyone because you don't want others stealing from you. You would not hurt or lie to others because you do not want others to do those things to you. Being honest and kind are the ways Jesus wants us to live with integrity.

"And as you wish that others would do to you, do so to them," Luke 6:31

Know this: **Living with integrity is easy when you think about being kind and truthful to others.** By living with integrity, you will also have a holy life.

Keeping Christ in Christmas

"Therefore the Lord himself will give you a sign. Behold, the virgin shall conceive and bear a son, and shall call his name Immanuel," Isaiah 7:14

The verse above is from the Old Testament that was written many years before Christ was born. Did you know that the birth of Christ was predicted more than 500 years before His birth? In fact, there are at least 10 prophecies in the Old Testament about the birth of Christ and many more predictions about what He would do here on earth. His birth was talked about for hundreds of years before He was born. The people of Israel knew that God would send a savior and they were excited about it for a long, long time.

When we celebrate the Advent Season in anticipation of the birthday of Christ, we count the season as the four Sundays before Christmas. Television ads, advertisements in stores and on the internet or newspapers, start in October! When we celebrate the Christmas season, it seems like a very long time before the day of Christmas arrives. But can you imagine waiting more than 500 years for the birth of Christ?

The people living during the Old Testament years were looking forward to the birth of Christ because they knew He would be sent from God and He would change the world for the better. When we think about Christmas today, the meaning is changed in our world. Christmas is now associated with presents, Santa Claus, and sales on items that begin months before Christmas. Christmas is also the time we go to parties, plan special events, travel all over to see families, and hope we get something special for a present.

But how can we keep Christ in Christmas? Take a look at this verse below:

> *"And she gave birth to her firstborn son and wrapped him in swaddling cloths and laid him in a manger, because there was no place for them in the inn," Luke 2:7*

Think about this verse. A woman, far away from her home, gives birth to a baby and there is nowhere for her, her new baby, and husband to sleep. Not only that, they are sleeping in a manager, with animals, and nothing for the new baby. These are very meager beginnings for the greatest person ever to walk the face of the earth. Perhaps we could remember these beginnings when we think of Christmas instead of thinking about shopping, parties, and hectic schedules. Here are some ideas to help you remember Christ: go to church on Christmas Eve and on Christmas day, go to special music programs or plays that are based on the birth of Christ, help your family prepare for the holidays by doing something extra without being asked to do it, offer to help others whom you may not know by donating toys, visit a nursing home to sing carols, play Christmas hymns and carols, sit with your family and tell them what you are thankful for this Christmas, just to name a few. And if you really want to be sure you keep Christ in Christmas, read the account of His birth given in the book of Luke. This is a beautiful account that will touch your heart-which is the real meaning of Christmas. Know this: **Christmas celebrates the birth of the Son of God, the greatest person ever to walk on earth.**

Christmas Giving from the Heart

"Each one must give as he has decided in his heart, not reluctantly or under compulsion, for God loves a cheerful giver"
2 Corinthians 9:7

Christmas is the happiest season of the year for many people. This is a time when you might make out a whole list of things you want other people to give to you. You do this because you know your family and friends truly love giving you presents. This is the highlight of the family members' holiday! You have probably had countless pictures taken of you holding up a new present for the relative, so they could take your picture. For really special presents, they may try to catch the reaction on your face as you open the package to see the surprise inside. They love seeing your happiness.

Likewise, as a growing Christian, you are reminded by Paul in his letter to the congregation in Corinth, that gifts, and the act of giving, are decided within the heart. You must decide what you will give to others. This does not mean you have to decide about spending lots of money on a present, but it does mean that, with a cheerful heart, you will give to others. It can be a present, a Christmas card, a chore that you do without being asked, a hard task that you know will help another, or any number of nice things in your heart that you want to do for someone else. It isn't just the fact that you gave that makes God happy, it is that you gave with a cheerful heart.

> *"Sell your possessions, and give to the needy. Provide yourselves with moneybags that do not grow old, with a treasure in the heavens that does not fall, where no thief approaches and no moth destroys. For where your treasure is, there will be your heart also" Luke 12:33-34*

At first, it looks like this verse is giving advice about you getting money and storing it up. That is not what this verse is about. We are reminded that the amount of money does not matter, it is that we pay attention to things other than money. It is an important statement about the low value of material things and money and the high value of your heart. What is important in your heart is where your real treasure will be. So, for people who only think about money, there is very little room left for love and other important feelings of the heart.

> *"The point is this: whoever sows sparingly will also reap sparingly, and whoever sows bountifully will also reap bountifully" 2 Corinthians 9:6*

When you think about the verse above and relate it to giving, it means that when you do not give of yourself, you will likely not receive much back. But when you give willingly and cheerfully from your heart, and you do so freely, you will receive much. Know this: **Giving at Christmas is not** about money or how many presents you get, it is about giving to others from your heart.

Your Best Effort

> *"Whatever you do, work heartily, as for the Lord and not for men…" Colossians 3:23*

> *"Brothers, I do not consider that I have made it my own. But one thing I do: forgetting what lies behind and straining forward to what lies ahead, I press on toward the goal for the prize of the upward call of God in Christ Jesus" Philippians 3:13-14*

We are asked to do many things each day. Homework, schoolwork, jobs, and chores, for example. We know we are to always put forth our best effort in everything we are asked to do by our teachers and our parents. And, most of the time, we take this seriously because the way we behave each day is a reflection of our beliefs and in the working of the Holy inspired Word within us. The verses above tell us to do all of our work to meet God's standards and not men's. That is not always what we are thinking when we are doing our homework or laundry. But, if we did think about these higher standards, we might go about our work more joyfully because we know that is how Jesus wants us to work.

But what about things you choose to do that are above the day-to-day routines? Suppose you are a member of a sports team and you are in a competition. You joined the team because you like the sport and now you are going to participate as a team member in a competition. This can make us nervous, and our minds might wander to worrying about how good we will be. The verse from Philippians above reminds us that we do nothing on our own without God. God is always there with us. We should keep our eye on the prize that is our reward when we do something to the glory of God.

The things we might choose to do may require that we meet some criterion to demonstrate that we are "good enough" to be able to participate in that activity. Now, this can really make us nervous. Why? Because we are too worried about the standards set before us by man and not by God. Here is the thing, when you focus on God's standard, trying to put your best effort toward the goal so you can glorify God, the other standards are actually not so scary. As the verses below tell us, we should not fear anything that is set by mankind. We should not have anxiety or dread because God will be with us. He will not leave us. And if we need more strength, more knowledge, more courage, He will give it to us when we ask.

"Be strong and courageous. Do not fear or be in dread of them, for it is the Lord your God who goes with you. He will not leave you or forsake you" Deuteronomy 31:6

"Finally, be strong in the Lord and in the strength of his might" Ephesians 6:10

Know this: **Standards set by mankind are beneath the standards of God so that believers who strive to work for God's glory will find the standards of men are not so scary.** Right before that competition, contest, or try out, close your eyes, say a quick prayer, and feel God's arms wrap around you.

The World Is Changing

"For everything there is a season, and a time for every matter under heaven," Ecclesiastes 3:1

You are living in a time and world of change. Your own world changes each day at school and home. Every day offers new opportunities and temptations. Some of the changes that happen can be hard. There are changes that might test your faith. For example, you find out your best friend is moving, your mom or dad needs to change jobs, or your favorite teacher is leaving during the middle of the year. These changes are not in your control, and you must adjust. Other changes are under your control. Examples of these are changing your school schedule next semester or changing your after-school job. You can weigh these out and look for Scripture to guide you. The verse below reminds us to always ask God, in good changes and unpredictable changes, and He will provide us with the wisdom to go the right direction when things change.

"If any of you lacks wisdom, let him ask God, who gives generously to all without reproach, and it will be given to him" James 1:5

No matter what else is going on in your life, you can always make a change to move closer to God. The first followers of Christ discovered they were changed by Jesus. They were born anew and began a brand-new relationship with God. Changing in this way, moving so close to God, is hard to understand. When the first followers tried to explain this, the listeners had difficulty understanding what the believers were talking about. It was indeed a mystery!

"Behold! I tell you a mystery. We shall not all sleep, but we shall all be changed" 1 Corinthians 15:51

"Do not marvel that I said to you, 'You must be born again'" John 3:7

Whether you are making good changes in your life or you have had some changes happen that were out of your control, each day can be a good day in Christ. When changes are troubling you, remember how much God loves you. Think long and hard about Jesus's love for you and His grace. Then remember this love as you go about your day.

"They are new every morning; great is your faithfulness" Lamentations 3:23

Know this: **The love that Jesus has for you will never change.** Even though your world may change in a way that makes your head spin, God is there, and the love and grace given by Jesus is always with you.

"Jesus Christ is the same yesterday and today and forever" Hebrews 13:8

Expectations and Disappointments

"For the gifts and the calling of God are irrevocable" Romans 11:29

You have been blessed with so many gifts from God. You are kind, loving, respectful, and have knowledge greater than you know. You have the Holy Spirit in your heart and mind and you love God the Father and Son. All of the gifts, talents, and blessings, are from God. No matter what might go wrong in your day, you know for certain that the gift of God's calling of your heart to Him will never be taken away.

"And the peace of God, which surpasses all understanding, will guard your hearts and minds in Christ Jesus," Philippians 4:7

The wonderful Holy Spirit will guard your heart. Whenever you experience a disappointment, it is the Holy Spirit that will lift you back up. With the Spirit within you, you can calm your fears and any anxieties that might pop up. So, you know that you rely on God and simply look forward.

"Trust in the Lord, and do good; dwell in the land and befriend faithfulness" Psalm 37:3

"Behold, God is my salvation; I will trust, and will not be afraid; for the Lord God is my strength and my song, and he has become my salvation" Isaiah 12:2

Each day you give your best in everything you do. When you put forth your best and things still don't work out, it is not a reflection on your skill or ability. It was just not the day for you to shine...yet. But with hope in your heart and your willingness to continue moving forward, you will meet your goals soon. Know this: **The Holy Spirit will point you to Jesus, and you will be lifted up again.**

Participating in Sports

"For while bodily training is of some value, godliness is of value in every way, as it holds promise for the present life and also for the life to come," 1 Timothy 4:8

"Do you not know that in a race all runners run, but only one receives the prize? So run that you may obtain it," 1 Corinthians 9:24

Students in school often become involved in team sports,[8] and individual sports, for a variety of reasons. Sports activities are excellent ways to meet friends and form relationships with your team members and your coach. Joining a sports team also provides a means of disciplining your body and mind because you are required to train regularly for an extended period of time. Sports competitions offer opportunities to achieve some level of competence by proving you have the abilities and skills to win in contests. When you win in a contest, it offers you recognition not only in the contest but afterward at school. These are all ways in which you grow physically, emotionally, and in your friendships.

With all of these positive reasons to become a member of a team and train to win competitions, the first verse above reminds us that there is something

---

[8] Does God Attend Sports Events?
https://christianpublishinghouse.co/2016/12/17/does-god-attend-sports-events/

even greater to train for and to achieve. The verse from 1 Timothy states that we benefit from training, we should be training our minds in godliness and showing others that we are striving to be better people. We work toward being better for our current time, for our future years, and when we eventually go to heaven. And the verse from Corinthians acknowledges that we can all be participants in the sports competitions, but only one will be the winner. In this letter to the people of Corinth, Paul tells us to always be working to be the best that we can be. He said to train and then run hard to win the final prize. When we think about our day-to-day living, we can remember to live our lives with holiness and always be thinking of the final prize with Jesus.

The verse below is a reminder that all competitions and all contests of life are only worth winning when we play by the rules. In Christian life, our rules are the ones we know from the Bible and especially what Jesus taught us about how we are to treat each other.

"An athlete is not crowned unless he competes according to the rules," 2 Timothy 2:5

And finally, when you do succeed in sports and in life, always be humble. Let others give you praise and recognition. You have heard people say it is important to be a good loser, but we are reminded by this verse that we should also be good winners! Being a good winner reflects Jesus's words about treating others how we want to be treated. We do not like hearing our friends brag when they beat us.

Likewise, we should not brag about our winnings but let others congratulate us and then express our thanks to them and to God.

> *"Let another praise you, and not your own mouth; a stranger, and not your own lips," Proverbs 27:2*

Know this: **In all you do, try your best, treat others fairly, and praise God for your successes.** Participating in sports is another way to train yourself for the future.

Grateful and Ungrateful

"A tranquil heart gives life to the flesh, but envy makes the bones rot" Proverbs 14:30

"Be still before the Lord and wait patiently for him; fret not yourself over the one who prospers in his way, over the man who carries out evil devices!" Psalm 37:7

You have heard the saying that compares a glass of water that is half full with a glass of water that is half empty. The reason this short comparison has been handed down for so many generations is because it makes a strong point: it is the same glass and it shows the difference is not in the amount of water, but in how you look at the glass. A person who sees the glass as half full might say "I still have a half of a glass!" as if to be grateful for the water in the glass. A person who says, "I only have half a glass!" is saying it in a way that indicates it is not enough or that they wish they had more in the glass or that they are afraid they are about to run out of water. We can look at the first person's view of the glass as half full and believe that they are grateful and appreciative for what they have. The second person is one who is not grateful for what is in the glass but wishes there was more. These two viewpoints are also described as one being optimistic or having a good outlook on life, and one being pessimistic or having an outlook of gloom, doom, ungratefulness, and envy.

We can carry this attitude of grateful and ungrateful throughout every aspect of our lives. A person with a grateful heart is one who is viewed as being thankful, loving, and kind. When we think of a person who is ungrateful throughout life, we think about a person is seems grumpy, unappreciative, and complains because they always want more. The verse above from Proverbs makes the comparison of these two types of people and notes that the person who is at peace with what they have seems to have a full life while the person who is not grateful will seem to wither away without having a full wonderful life. The second verse tells us to be patient and not to be concerned about those who seem to have everything by their own devices rather than through God. In other words, we should not be envious of those who have a lot of material things. We should be patient and always be thinking about God rather than people who seem to have everything worldly.

"Therefore let us be grateful for receiving a kingdom that cannot be shaken, and thus let us offer to God acceptable worship, with reference and awe" Hebrews 12:28

The verse from Hebrews tells us to always be grateful first for our belief in God, we are children of His kingdom. This will never change. God will always be there for us and we should stay strong in our faith. This same verse reminds us that we should worship God first and that this worship is above all else worldly.

"But seek first the kingdom of God and his righteousness, and all these things will be added to you" Matthew 6:33

The verse from Matthew above states that seeking God first is all we need. If we strive to have a close relationship with God, we will not be envious or ungrateful. We will be grateful for everything we have in life. We will always know that being one of God's children is the most important thing in life and because we will have a grateful heart, we will not want anything else. And, if we have a faith that is this strong, God will add blessings to our lives. Know this: **Staying near to God is the most important thing we can do and, by doing this, He will bless your life.**

Understanding Others

"A fool takes no pleasure in understanding, but only in expressing his opinion," Proverbs 18:2

"Whoever restrains his words has knowledge, and he who has a cool spirit is a man of understanding" Proverbs 17:27

We have all had friends or family members tell us things they were thinking or worrying about. When you hear their remarks, what do you do? What are you expected to do? Often, you may want to jump right in a begin telling them where they went wrong or what they should have done. Sometimes, we find ourselves doing this before the other person has finished telling us the whole story. As the verse from Proverbs states above, we are foolish if we express our opinions quickly. We should listen to everything the person tells us before we say anything. Sometimes your friends will simply want to "vent" or just express their anger, sadness, or excitement. They may not be looking for an opinion or for someone to give advice. So, what should you do when they begin telling their story? As stated above, a person who has a "cool spirit," who does not react initially but weighs things out and carefully considers all sides, is a person considered to have understanding. It is also wise to wait and see if the person requests advice after they have completed their statements. If they should ask what you would do, it is important to carefully consider all sides and then to especially consider, as a Christian, the actions your friend might need to take.

There is something even more important than listening. When you hear or see a loved one or family member who has had an experience that upsets them, the more important thing we can do is have empathy. Empathy means that you feel as they feel. You are walking in their shoes. As the verse below points out, if your friend or family member is rejoicing, rejoice with them. If they are crying, you cry with them. This is understanding at the deepest level.

"Rejoice with those who rejoice, weep with those who weep." Romans 12:15

Why is empathy so important? In the verse from Ephesians below, we are instructed to be kind and tenderhearted but also, we are told to forgive one another. In other words, we should have empathy for our friend who perhaps became angry with us. When they explain their side, listen deeply. Understand and have empathy. Then you tell the person you forgive them. Jesus showed us the greatest example of empathy ever displayed. Jesus was the human expression of God. As a human, He also had empathy and understood all sides of our human issues. He understood how hard it is to refrain from sinning. But, when we do sin, His empathy for us is why He died on the cross for us. Know this: **Jesus loves us so much that He listens, understands and forgives.**

"Be kind to one another, tenderhearted, forgiving one another, as God in Christ forgave you," Ephesians 4:32

OTHER RELEVANT BOOKS

Christian Publishing House
ISBN-13: 978-1-945757-92-1
ISBN-10: 1-945757-92-2

Christian Publishing House

ISBN-13: 978-1-945757-47-1

ISBN-10: 1-945757-47-7

Terry Overton

Christian Publishing House

ISBN-13: 978-1-945757-60-0

ISBN-10: 1-945757-60-4

For I delight in the law of God, in my inner being, but I see in my members another law waging war against the law of my mind and making me captive to the law of sin that dwells in my members.—The Apostle Paul (Rom. 7:22-23)

WAGING WAR

A Christian's Cognitive Behavioral Therapy Workbook

Heather Freeman

Christian Publishing House

ISBN-13: 978-1-945757-42-6

ISBN-10: 1-945757-42-6

GOD WILL GET YOU
THROUGH THIS
Hope and Help for
Your Difficult Times

EDWARD D. ANDREWS

Christian Publishing House
ISBN-13: 978-1-945757-72-3

ISBN-10: 1-945757-72-8

FEARLESS

Be Courageous and Strong Through
Your Faith In These Last Days

EDWARD D. ANDREWS

Christian Publishing House
ISBN-13: 978-1-945757-69-3

ISBN-10: 1-945757-69-8

Christian Publishing House

ISBN-13: 978-1-945757-74-7

ISBN-10: 1-945757-74-4

Christian Publishing House
ISBN-13: 978-1-945757-73-0

ISBN-10: 1-945757-73-6

Terry Overton

Christian Publishing House

ISBN-13: 978-1-945757-86-0

ISBN-10: 1-945757-86-8

Author of Over 75 Books

PROMISES OF GOD'S GUIDANCE

God Show Me Your Ways, Teach Me Your
Paths, Guide Me In Your Truth and Teach Me

EDWARD D. ANDREWS

Christian Publishing House
ISBN-13: 978-1-945757-87-7

ISBN-10: 1-945757-87-6

Terry Overton

Author of Over 75 Books

BLESSED BY GOD IN SATAN'S WORLD

How All Things Are
Working for Your Good

EDWARD D. ANDREWS

Christian Publishing House
ISBN-13: 978-1-945757-88-4

ISBN-10: 1-945757-88-4

Christian Publishing House
ISBN-13: 978-1-945757-62-4

ISBN-10: 1-945757-62-0

Terry Overton

CHRISTIAN
APOLOGETIC EVANGELISM

REACHING HEARTS WITH THE
ART OF PERSUASION

All Christians Are Scripturally Obligated to
Evangelize—Matt. 24:14; 28:19-20; Ac 1:8

EDWARD D. ANDREWS

Christian Publishing House
ISBN-13: 978-1-945757-75-4

ISBN-10: 1-945757-75-2

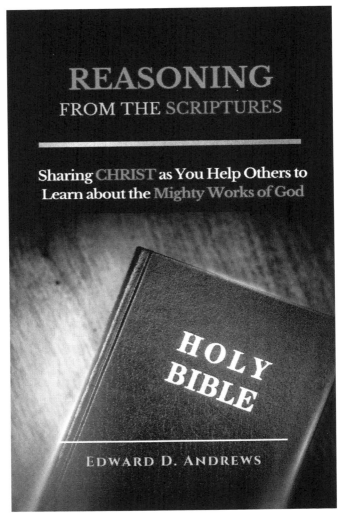

Christian Publishing House

ISBN-13: 978-1-945757-82-2

ISBN-10: 1-945757-75-2

Made in the USA
Lexington, KY
12 October 2018